MY FAVORITE SPORT

BASEBALL

Nancy Streza

xist Publishing

Published in the United States by Xist Publishing
www.xistpublishing.com
PO Box 61593 Irvine, CA 92602

First Edition
ISBN: 9781532406416
eISBN: 9781532406423

Table of Contents

The batter steps up to the plate. The pitcher winds up. Crack! The ball is hit and the batter starts running.

I love to play baseball!

Baseball is an American game where two teams try to score runs to win.

Baseball is played on a field. The infield is shaped like a diamond. It has four bases: first base, second base, third base, and home plate. The outfield is a large space of grass that ends with a fence.

A baseball game has nine innings. During each inning, each team has a turn to bat and a turn to field. In most baseball games, everyone on the team takes turns being up to bat.

A baseball game has
how many innings?

Check and see if you're right at the end of this book!

When it is the team's turn to be on the field, everyone plays a different position. The pitcher throws the ball to the batter.

If the batter hits the ball, he will run around the bases to try and score a run. The players on the field will try and stop him.

A batter can also get out if he does not hit the ball. Missing a fair pitch is called a strike. After three strikes, the batter is out.

The batter can also get out if someone in the field catches his hit before it touches the ground. This is called a "fly ball."

Do You Remember?

How many strikes does a batter get?

Check and see if you're right at the end of this book!

After a team gets three outs, they are done batting. It is the other team's turn to try and score.

Baseball players wear hats and use gloves to catch the ball. Batters always wear a helmet to stay safe.

Do You Remember?

How many outs does a team have?

Check and see if you're right at the end of this book!

Baseball players practice batting, throwing, catching and running. They will also practice fielding the ball and throwing it to the right base so they can get the batters out.

What's your favorite thing about baseball?

Glossary

Infield : The part of a baseball field where the bases are.

Outfield : The part of a baseball field furthest from batter.

Fly Ball : A hit baseball that is in the air not touching the ground.

Run : The term used for a score in baseball.

Strike : A missed pitch that is in the strike zone.

Inning : A section of time in the game consisting of each team having a turn at bat.

Did You Remember?

Answers:
Question #1:
There are 9 innings in a baseball game.
Question #2:
A batter can receive up to 2 strikes before he or she is out.
Question #3:
In baseball, there are 3 outs.

Made in the USA
Monee, IL
23 October 2022

16448307R00021